I0462223

More Clients Now!

The Beauty Pros Marketing Guide.

Explode Your Clientele, Maximize Your
Bookings To Make A 6 Figure Income.

Sade Lorelle

Copyright © 2016 Sade Lorelle

All rights reserved.

BROWVANA LLC.

ISBN-10: 1541210662
ISBN-13: 978-1541210660

DEDICATION

Dedicated to all the Eyebrow Microblading
Artist, Eyelash Extension Technician,
Hairstylist, Massage Therapist or beauty
professional bold enough to make their
dreams a reality.

CONTENTS

INTRODUCTION

Let's keep this short and sweet. I'm Sade Lorelle licensed esthetician, cosmetic tattooist, electrologist, and trainer. I've been involved in aesthetics for about 10 years. I left the industry to pursue a career in sales, where I eventually became a sales supervisor and trainer. I learned so much about client psychology and client acquisition; I decided to return to beauty industry to hit it harder than ever but also share my knowledge. This guide book should spark your creativity and increase your clientele books. This book is not full of filler or fluff, mainly because I hate that. This is all meat and straight to the point. So let's jump in, let's find you some clients.

1
GET STARTED
DOMAIN NAMES AND
WEBSITES

From this day forward you are now a brand. How do you intend to brand yourself and your company? You've done the training you've gotten the certificate, and you have the tools, unleash the clients, right? Wrong! Knowing how to do your chosen skill of is very, very important. In fact, if you are unable to do professional quality work put down this book and go practice. Take your craft seriously either do it with passion or not at all! Your work should speak for you by its quality.

Jumping right in you need a website. This is the 21st century, and everyone must have an online presence, word of mouth is everything in this business but so is your web footprint. It's not always the best practitioner with the most clients it's the professional who has the most exposure. Stretching your exposure will maximize your income tenfold. So let's talk about choosing a name for your company. Now here are several options here some people love to use their names example Kim's Lashes, okay. But here's the problem with that who in the hell is Kim and why would your clients care about Kim. You must understand the psychology of your clientele. Unless you already have a large social media following under your name don't use your name. Now if you do great, you have less work cut out for you. You already have eyes set on you now it's just learning how to harness your influence to place money in your pocket.

While choosing a name you want it to be obvious to your customer, just by seeing it they should have an idea of what kind of services you do. However obvious but not boring guys or generic. Nothing like Good Massages, not eye catching enough. You want something memorable. My method is this I take to the internet; I have a sheet of paper and my pen. I like to choose one word that would be a benefit to my customer, and the 2nd word will describe my service. So if I am a Brow Professional I would write a line down the center of my page and in my left column or word 1 side I would write beautiful and on the other side I would write brows. Now by searching the meaning of beautiful, I get the definition which is pleasing the senses or mind aesthetically. As well as great synonyms such as attractive, pretty, handsome, alluring, lovely, charming, delightful, appealing, ravishing, gorgeous, stunning, glamorous, bewitching, graceful, elegant, exquisite, aesthetic, artistic, decorative, magnificent; divine, drop-dead gorgeous, killer, cute, foxy. A lot of great words also I would suggest possibly translating the word into a foreign language as long as it's a commonly understood word such as Bella which is Italian for beautiful. You may also choose to combine to words together to create one creative word as long as it is still easily understood. This is the route I took by combing the word nirvana, meaning perfect harmony and the word eyebrow to conjure Browvana, my microblading company. Word of caution though does not choose a word that is not used in everyday speech because no one is going to know what you're talking about. Interesting but not undefinable.

Domain Names

Next, you're going to want to make sure that the name you have chosen is available for a domain name. A domain name is simply the name for your website. Stick to .com's only. No dashes, no underscores and no names over 11 letters as your main domain name. You want a top shelf domain. I also advise against getting those pricy domains that are like $10,000; we are not trying to waste money here. I suggest no .biz, .mia, .net or any of those other extensions the reason why is that .com's place better in search engines like Google. If you have dashes or underscore it reads as a scam possibly to Google which will hurt your ranking as well, so stay away from those. If the name you like is not available, you may want to choose something else because your domain name is a vital part of your brand. These are usually inexpensive under $20 I recommend either Godaddy or 1 and 1. Once you have your domain, you will want to set up a matching email. I'm sorry but I find your businessname@gmail.com so tacky, it doesn't look professional at all. Go ahead and spend the extra $2 to $5 and get an email address that matches your domain through your domain provider. Don't be cheap.

Websites and Finding Help

Once you have your domain name and your email. Get a website platform I love Shopify it's super easy to use and set up even if you are not a professional. Their templates are clean and user-friendly. There are so many apps to plug into your website that will allow you to run a more efficient business. There are apps for scheduling appointments, referral programs, shipping products, etc. If you are not very tech savvy at all the help can be easily found online through outsourcing. I suggest fiverr you can find many professionals all over the world to design your Shopify site for a bargain. Many services are professional quality and as the name suggest as low as $5!

You want to make sure you have a logo something that embodies your brand you can find a fiverr pro to design this for you for $5. Make sure to receive jpg. ,which is a common image file and png. files which have a transparent backing, these files are great for ads, merchandise, etc. Once you receive your logo with transparent backing you need cards, a lot of them! I suggest keeping some in your bag at all times just in case an opportunity to network or advertise your brand arises. Many beauty stores allow you to leave cards at the checkout, make sure you take that opportunity.

Color Psychology

When you select, the design and colors for your brand be aware of color psychology. In general terms, bright, bold colors grab attention, just don't overdo it. Soft tones send a more sophisticated image, but are so subtle may be overlooked. Here are the general meaning of different colors in society...

Red suggests passion, energy, danger or aggression; warmth and heat. Choosing red for your logo can make it feel more dynamic. If you are looking for more sex appeal for your brand, use red. Red is also a great color for your book now buttons on your website or some shade of red.

Orange is usually seen as the color of innovation and modern thinking. It also carries connotations of youth, fun, affordability, and approachability.

Yellow requires cautious use as it has some negative connotations including its signifying of cowardice and its use in warning signs.

However, it is sunny, warm and friendly.

Green is commonly used when a company desires to emphasize their natural and ethical credentials, like being organic, think Whole Foods. Other meanings credited to it include growth and freshness, and it's popular with health services too. If your company has a holistic approach green would be great especially for massage and skincare business.

Blue is one of the most widely used colors in for logos. It implies professionalism, serious-mindedness, honesty, sincerity, and calm. Blue is also connected with authority and success. Blue makes people trust which is why many healthcare companies use blue.

Purple speaks to us of royalty and luxury. It has long been associated with wisdom and dignity, and has been known as the color of creative, fantasy, unconventional and riches.

Black is a color with a split meaning. On the one side, it implies power and sophistication, but on the other side it is linked with wickedness and death. You will want will probably need a black and white version for use in media in which color is not available. If you want your company to appear more upscale black will give that image luxury to your brand.

White is generally associated with hygiene,

cleanliness, simplicity and innocence.

Brown has masculine associations and is often used for products associated with country life and the outdoors.

Pink can be fun and flirty, but its feminine associations mean it is often dodged for products or service not specifically targeted at women.

These associations are not the unbending rule, but they're good to keep in mind as you make your color choices.

Buying Related Domain Names, Keywords and SEO

To assist with your search engine optimization aka SEO, you may want to buy several domains that can redirect to your webpage. These domain names should either relate to customer benefit (e.g., low prices or expertise) or location (state or city). For example, if Lovely Lashes is located in Atlanta, Georgia and specializes in mink lash extensions you may want to purchase domain such as Atlantalashes.com, minklashesatlanta.com or cheaplashextensions.com. These are the keywords that your audience is looking for and so these are the words you want as your related domains hat you can redirect to your main page. Google Trends can show you what your target audience is searching and what are the related searches. Use these searches as domain names and keywords for your website to drive traffic. Use a blog to write an article on one of the most searched questions related to your profession. Pack this article full of commonly searched questions and topics. If your clients are looking for answers you have them, this makes you an authority in your field and a trusted person in your area in your specialty.

2
CREATING YOUR OWN
MARKETING MATERIALS

Once you have your logo in hand, you can now start slapping your logo across your website, business card, flyers and really whatever you like. I personally use Canva to create many of my marketing materials it's mainly free to use unless you use one of their images which is only a dollar. Canva is very simple to use, and you can create some beautiful designs for Web or print: blog graphics, presentations, Facebook covers, flyers, posters, invitations and so forth.

I also strongly suggest making a car magnet

for your vehicle and if you have employees buy them one too. It doesn't cost much to turn your vehicle into a mobile ad for your services. Make sure to include a before and after picture on your car magnet to highlight your skill. Keep the design simple, clean yet informative. If your service is kind of unusual, educate your future client. By including one informative sentence of what your service is and what the benefit is, this will really help the phones ring. Include your logo, information sentence (if necessary), before and after picture, ways to contact phone number social media and address. I recommend UPrinting to create your car magnets. Just stick it on when you are ready to roll.

Once you have the designs ready from Canva if you made your own or Fiverr if you hired a pro, get everything printed. You can get your designs printed through UPrinting, your cards, poster brochures, etc.

If your location is near a busy intersection print up a sign to stick outside. Make it a sale or a free consultation, remember it needs to be a benefit to client give them a reason to come inside. Aby the way make sure all of your designs are consistent, similar colors similar designs this reinforces your brand. Check with your city's advertising laws some

areas may fine you for placing a sign outside.
here.

3
SOCIAL MEDIA AND INFLUENCERS

Be sure to snag all social media with matching names claim your YouTube, Instagram, Facebook business page, printerest, twitter, and snapchat. Even if you don't plan to use all of these media outlets claim them just in case you decide to in the future. So if your company is BrowBella all of your social media should be the same. Also be consistent in capitalization and spacing, this helps for web searches. So don't do this Instagram BROW_BELLA, Facebook Brow-Bella and YouTube BrowBellaWax make them all the same consistency.

Design your business pages to flow with the rest of your branding. Plug in your social media to your website with buy buttons or book now buttons. Shopify has this capacity. Consult an expert or customer service to assist you if needed.

Sponsored Ads

Facebook and Instagram are great for beauty businesses you can easily boost a post across both platforms for as little as $5 a day. Be sure to edit your target audience by location, age, and gender. This is a great tool to highlight your work or promote a sale.

Create Facebook offers. You only pay for the promotion of the ad you can easily include a coupon code for online or in-store discounts, and you keep the entire profit from these sales, these should also be targeted.

Pinterest for Products

If you sell products, plug your Pinterest into your website, so potential customers can click an image on Pinterest and be redirected to your website. There are various websites on Shopify to assist you with monetizing your Pinterest.

Instagram Growth Tips

Use clear photographs and popular filters for beauty and fashion use the following filters 1. Kelvin, 2. Valencia and 3. Nashville. For a client selfie's 1. Normal, 2. Slumber, 3. Skyline. Keep in mind the most popular filter overall is Clarendon. Study your competition reviews their Instagram pages what is heir headlines and hashtags. Take those hashtags and then comment on your own post. Then make another comment with the most used hashtags. Here are some you may want to include.

Most Popular Hashtags

#popular #instagood #photooftheday #instamood #picoftheday #bestoftheday #instadaily #igdaily #instagramhub #instacool #me #photo #instagram #teamfollowback #followback #instafollow #instagood #love #me #tbt #cute #follow #followme #happy #tagforlikes #beautiful #self #girl #like4like #smile #friends #fun #like #fashion #summer #instadaily #igers #instalike #slay #amazing #tflers #follow4follow #bestoftheday #likeforlike #instamood #style #wcw #family #141 #f4f #nofilter #lol #life #pretty #repost #hair #my #sun #webstagram #iphoneonly #art

#tweegram #cool #followback #instafollow
#instasize #bored #instacool #funny #mcm
#instago #instasize #girls #party #music
#eyes #nature #beauty #night #fitness
#look #nice #sky #christmas #baby

Instagram Good Habits

With Instagram follow all your suggested
people and follow your competition's
followers especially if they are within the same
state as you, you share a customer base.
Engage you customers with questions. Like
which one is your favorite and double tap if
you agree. Also simply following a lot of
people will automatically boost your followers
some of which will convert into clients.

**Influencers, Spokespersons, Brand
Ambassadors and Vloggers**

People will follow the lead of their favorite
person, harness the power of their exposure
to expand your book. Post ads on modeling
and acting websites for a cast calling offering
free services for a select few to represent the
company. You are looking for someone with
several thousand engaged followers. You may
also want to provide this person with a
referral affiliate link so they can include in
their bio and be paid for the referrals. This

should motivate your spokesperson to spread the word to their already engaged audience. Sponsors who are sexually explicit or inappropriate for a brand you will want to stay clear of so they don't hurt the image of your company. Vloggers are also great, encourage my experience videos and make sure they link your company's info in the descriptions. Also, encourage your customers to do the same if they want to do my experience video, it's great exposure for your company.

There are various ways to find influencers for your company I recommend posting ads on ModelMayhem, Craigslist, Fiverr and Famefind just to name a few. Many influencers are looking for an opportunity to monetize their social media following. Some will even produce a video for you for as low as $50.

Infographics

You can have an infographic created from Fiverr to educate your client. These visual images charts or diagram used to represent information and you can spread these images across your Instagram, Facebook, and other social platforms.

Contest, Giveaways and Charity Work

Running a contest and doing giveaways are another great way to spread the word of your services. Create personalized #hashtags for these contests and have the contestants like and share your post. Make sure all your photographs have been watermarked with your company name or logo to avoid image theft. If your specialty can help a specific disadvantage group, contact a local group or support group and offer a special discount for group members.

4
REFERRAL PROGRAMS & FINANCING OPTIONS

Referral Programs

Referral Candy is a Shopify App that allows you to turn every customer into a referral source through either discounted rates or cash rewards. The way it works is that the referral source signs up online, links their PayPal account and shares their customized link. The current rate for this service is under $30. They will track and pay out your referrers based on the timeframe you requested. An example of a program you could start would offer $15 off for the service and $35 referral reward fee. Adjust these rates depending on the cost for your services. Limited the reward fees to first-time customers and first service only. Share the first visit and keep the rest.

Do bring a friend discounts to encourage multiple bookings. An example of this would-be eyebrow microblading normally $397 book with a friend to save $75 each! You can also offer lash parties, brow parties, teeth whiting parties, etc. Whatever your niche is, offer a discount for booking as a group.

Sharable carts or checkouts encourage your clients to share their bookings at checkout. Offer them $5 off to do so, and you've just gained more exposure.

Special Discounts

Creating special coupon codes for holidays (New Years, Xmas, Black Friday and Valentine's Day), special groups (e.g. Military personnel), College Student pricing, etc. Get creative to get them through your door.

Shared Profits and Deep Discounts (Style Seat, Yelp, and Groupon)

Style Seat is the online space for beauty & wellness professionals and clients. As a professionals, you can showcase your work, connect with new and existing clients. They take about a 50% commission from your bookings on the first visit. You may want to use this for free consultation services to avoid giving away profits especially if you are in a specialty with limited visits. This service allows you to possibly capture more clients and can even help with bookings if you choose to turn on the booking feature. You're mainly there just for the exposure.

Groupon will bring in the clients and the calls. Groupon has no upfront cost but rather takes around a 50% commission for the clients that they find for you. If you are just getting started this is a nice resource to get your portfolio built up. You will see your daily views increase on your website. Once you have already a client base you may still want to use Groupon to drive traffic but minimize a number of available deals, it defaults at 20 but calls into scale that back, so you are conserving your profits. Also, offer a sale on your website that is at least 20% higher than the Groupon price but still a bargain so individuals who have visited the site but missed the Groupon will still book with you. Yelp also has a similar service to Groupon with no upfront cost to create a deal, and they take a smaller commission amount of around 30%. However, the Yelp deals tend to be less popular than Groupon's.

Financing Options

Sometimes people really love your work, but simply cannot find a way to afford your service or products. Now this is your job to find a way for them to get it there are apps such as Parti.ly which allows the customer to pay on a payment plan; I only recommend this for very pricey items and don't render any services until they have paid in full. Futurepay is another great resource which finances the product into smaller manageable payments as low as $25. This service is only available for products, not services. Now for services United Medical Credit will finance beauty procedures without being a doctor but the service must be at least $1000 and client must use this balance within 60 days. This one is perfect for procedures such as scalp pigmentation.

5
SHARED PROFITS AND DEEP DISCOUNTS

Shared Profits and Deep Discounts (Style Seat, Yelp, and Groupon)

Style Seat is the online space for beauty & wellness professionals and clients. As a professionals, you can showcase your work, connect with new and existing clients. They take about a 50% commission from your bookings on the first visit. You may want to use this for free consultation services to avoid giving away profits especially if you are in a specialty with limited visits. This service allows you to possibly capture more clients and can even help with bookings if you choose to turn on the booking feature. You're mainly there just for the exposure.

Groupon will bring in the clients and the calls. Groupon has no upfront cost but rather takes around a 50% commission for the clients that they find for you. If you are just getting started this is a nice resource to get your portfolio built up. You will see your daily views increase on your website. Once you have already a client base you may still want to use Groupon to drive traffic but minimize a number of available deals, it defaults at 20 but calls into scale that back, so you are conserving your profits. Also, offer a sale on your website that is at least 20% higher than the Groupon price but still a bargain so individuals who have visited the site but missed the Groupon will still book with you.

Yelp also has a similar service to Groupon with no upfront cost to create a deal, and they take a smaller commission amount of around 30%. However, the Yelp deals tend to be less popular than Groupon's.

6
GETTING PUBLICITY & DIRECTORIES

Add your business details to various local directories below is a list of the top 50 directories.

Online Local Business Directories/Listings for Local Marketing

Google, Bing, Yahoo!, Yelp, Facebook, Better Business Bureau, Angie's List, Merchant Circle, LinkedIn, YP.com, Whitepages, Superpages.com, Yellowbook, CitySearch, MapQuest/Yext, Local.com, Foursquare, CitySlick, USDirectory.com, Dex Media, BizJournals.com, TeleAtlas, Discover

Our Town, EZ Local, Kudzu, CityVoter, Manta, UsCity, Advice Local, InfoUSA, MojoPages, Brownbook, Magic Yellow, CitySquares, TripAdvisor, Thumbtack, ShowMeLocal, Hotfrog, Brownbook and InsiderPages. List with these sites for FREE don't pay for the upgraded features it's not necessary. If you prefer to not manually input these listings you can usually get listed in multiple directories through your domain provider.

Presence and Reviews

Craigslist, Thumbtack, Yelp if you don't have them, get them. Don't overlook Craigslist as a place to post your services; people will call you. As far as thumbtack this is an online service that matches customers with local professionals. Your clients can leave a review which helps your credibility and your likelihood to be booked. Yelp is composed of user reviews and recommendations of top services; many people rely on this service to view your client photos and read actual client feedback. Customer service and quality work are vital here.

Getting Publicity

Getting your company featured in a

magazine or publication can be great for your image. Being a featured company will advertise your brand, build your credibility and give you immediate expertise. Getting in a popular magazine can be the luck of the draw. Lucky for us you don't have to be that lucky, it's a matter of being aware of the resources. Help a reporter out also known as HARO journalists with a source for upcoming stories and daily opportunities for sources to secure valuable media coverage. Many major publications such as Allure Magazine scout for sources directly from this site. A basic membership is free. It is just a matter of combing through the request and responding that simple. There's a few under sites with a similar service such as Source Bottle which is also a free online service that connects journalists with sources.

7
GOOGLE ADWORDS, DIRECT MAIL AND NETWORKING

If you haven't heard of it, you may have been living under a rock. Millions of companies rely on Google AdWords to market their brands. There are no budget minimums; you can advertise on mobile devices, YouTube and help your clients find you. There are various styles of ads available from search ads, banner ads, video ads, mobile ads and app ads. It's the most popular pay per click or PPC platform because it fits nearly any business and is entirely customizable to your needs and goals. Setting up an account is easy. To create an AdWords account, go to adwords.google.com and click "Start Now." Simply enter a valid email address, your website's URL, and create a password to get started. Once you create your first campaign, Google will ask for your billing information to keep on file. At the campaign level, you create a group of ads related to one specific goal or category, set a budget, and determine your target audience. To get set up and running quickly contact a Google AdWords Specialist.

Direct Mail Marketing

As a small business owner, you need to obtain new customers but may not know how to find them. Here are some basic direct mail marketing tips to simplify the process of generating leads and converting them into new clients. Firstly, who is your target customers? Knowing who your customers are is a crucial factor in direct marketing. You should know your customers' basic demographics, such as females 35 to 60 or females with children. Yet, understanding your customer's preferences like what is their shopping and purchasing attitudes. What trends do like, and products; or their lifestyle behaviors can help you become more efficient in the messages you'll use to communicate with your potential clients. Once you understand your audience, you can create a mailing list. The direct mail piece you create will reflect your company's message. The mailing piece signifies who, what you are and what you can do for the client. Make it consistent with what your overall brand. Quality is key your direct mail piece needs to reflect your professionalism.

There are various ways to run a direct mail marketing campaign from post cards to coupon by mail. Do be advised that the postcard route does tend to be quite pricey.

Social Networking

Networking goes side by side with a successful business. Networking is all about relationship building. Keep your conversation enjoyable, light and casual. You just want to get a conversation started. People want to do business with people they enjoy. If a potential client asks you about your service, be prepared with a simple description of what you do. A good practice is to have a few pictures and highlights of your service mentality prepared. Leave a lasting impression, tell people why you were inspired to start your company. Remember to smile and make people feel special. You should look people in the eye, say their names and listen to them. Be conversational, don't steamroll them with a one-sided conversation, give and take. At the end of your encounter ask for the best way to stay in touch. Exchange your cards, email, phone numbers or business social networks. Remember to follow up otherwise the effort goes to waste. Join local business groups and seek out networking opportunity. There are some websites like meetup.com that may allow you to introduce yourself and your services to a new audience.

8
CLIENT DATABASE AND ABANDON CARTS

Client Databases

A customer database can provide some great client info as far as ages of your customers, locations, and buying trends. It's a great learning resource. This data is the perfect tool to help you spot trends, your popular services or products. This will help you with your future marketing efforts.

Your client database also allows you to double dip for gold as well. Send Happy Birthday and Happy Holidays messages. Offer a special price for the upcoming birthday or holiday, get them back in the doors. 10% on your birthday, make those phones ring. It's a small act, but it does make a big difference. If you are in services like eyebrow microblading send touch up reminder early booking discounts. An example of this would be your almost ready for a touchup book now and save 15%, motivate your clients not to procrastinate.

Abandon Carts

Sometimes people visit but do not complete now I encourage you to allow customers to create an account that way; it's easier to track the cart abandoners. Don't make it a requirement just an option, now if they filled in enough details as far as their email, send them a coupon to book now and make it expire in a week. If they don't take the bait, send them periodic email reminders that offer a small discount to encourage their booking now. Their apps are available to assist with abandon cart acquisition.

9
LOYALTY PROGRAMS, SUBSCRIPTIONS AND CUSTOMER SERVICE.

Loyalty programs and Subscription
Offer packages and discounts for good behavior. If your clients need your services frequently, set up discounted member pricing and non- member pricing at a higher rate. Make your clients see the benefit of buying a package of services since it will save them 20% to buy 6 and advance. Or offer to buy 5 lash refills and get one free. You may even want to set up a subscription service to draft automatically ever month for these programs;

Shopify has apps that can help you manage this seamlessly.

Good Customer Service & Gift Giving

As we reach the end of this guide, I want to touch on the importance of providing good customer service to leave a lasting and professional impression. Doing great work with a terrible attitude will turn off clients who would want to rebook with you. Check your attitude at the door this is your business, wow them and make them feel great. To leave a great and memorable touch, I recommend little gifts be it a little gift bag with a chocolate and some business cards. This will make them feel special, and it turns your happy client into your sales person.

Word Of Mouth Is Everything In This Business, Let's Get Paid!

10
RESOURCES

I offer remote marketing analysis and phone/e-mail consultations for your small beauty business. At browvana.com, under the consulting tab.

Shopify
http://1.shopifytrack.com/aff_c?offer_id=2&aff_id=16450

Uprinting
http://www.uprinting.com/

Godaddy

www.godaddy.com

1 and 1
https://www.1and1.com/

Fiverr
https://www.fiverr.com/

Canva
https://www.canva.com/

Famebit
https://famebit.com/

Model Mayhem
https://www.modelmayhem.com

"A man's mind may be likened to a garden, which may be intelligently cultivated or allowed to run wild; but whether cultivated or neglected, it must, and will, bring forth. If no useful seeds are put into it, then an abundance of useless weed seeds will fall therein, and will continue to produce their kind."

— James Allen, As a Man Thinketh

www.ingramcontent.com/pod-product-compliance
Lightning Source LLC
Chambersburg PA
CBHW021416170526
45164CB00002B/676